Fred Edrissi

W9-BOB-616

Chef's Healthy Pasta

**Vegetarian
recipes to boost
your vitality
and health**

**alive
books**

Vancouver
Canada

C o n t e n t s

All About Pasta

Delicious Pasta Recipes

All About Pasta

Chi mangia solo, crepa solo,
chi mangia in compangnia,
vive in allegria.

Who eats alone dies alone,
who eats in company
lives in happiness.

Introduction . . . .

When the legendary tenor Luciano Pavarotti sings *O sole mio* before a hundred thousand opera fans, he is probably not thinking about pasta. However, after every performance, he returns to his hotel suite where a fully operational kitchen has been installed, and he prepares delicious pasta variations for his friends and fellow performers. Even when he is not on tour, he enjoys his favorite food in his North Italian hometown of Modena amongst his family and friends.

While Pavarotti may be the most famous admirer of pasta, he is certainly not the only one! There is no other food that has experienced such a triumphant conquest around the world. Also, there is hardly any food that has so many variations and can be combined with so many other things. Indeed, an entire national cuisine is built around this simple and nutritious food!

I have to admit, in all the years I have been a chef and a restaurateur, I've never had so much fun with my work than in writing this cookbook. Like Pavarotti, I am a huge fan of pasta and the Italian cuisine, which has endless variations. For this reason, I want to share my favorite recipes, which I have collected and created during my twenty years as a chef. As you prepare and enjoy these meals, I hope that you, your family and friends will experience this most important part of *la dolce vita!*

Bueno appetito!

What Is So Healthy About Pasta? . . . . .

Whole-wheat pasta is easy to digest and delivers as much energy as pure protein.

On one hand the starch contained in whole-wheat flour is a complex carbohydrate that is metabolized slowly by the body and delivers a sustained supply of energy, as much as energy as pure protein. On the other hand, pasta is easy to digest and gives you a feeling of satisfaction, which means you won't be hungry again in an hour.

The protein in pasta contains six to eight amino acids that are essential for the metabolism. To prepare a meal that is rich in protein, just add a little bit of Parmesan or pecorino cheese. Beyond that, pasta contains niacin, thiamin, riboflavin, calcium, iron and, if the pasta consists of whole grains of wheat, amaranth, Kamut®, spelt or quinoa, it will have plenty of roughage, commonly referred to as "fiber."

With a carefully considered choice of sauces, vegetables, a fresh green salad and perhaps a fruit dessert, you can create a perfectly healthy and delicious meal.

Where Does Pasta Come From? . . . . . .

Archaeologists have proven that the ancient Greeks and Romans cut thin, flat pasta into strips, which were quite similar to the pasta noodles we know today. The Arabs developed a method of winding the noodles around thin sticks and drying them in the open air.

Horace (65–8 BC), one of ancient Rome's greatest poets, described in great detail the pleasure he experienced with one dish made of noodles, chickpeas and leek.

Apicius, a Roman gourmet who lived in the first century AD, is often cited as the first author of a cookbook. Even at this early date, he wrote about preparing noodle-gratin and other pasta dishes in his work De Re Coquinaria (published in English as Roman Cookery).

For a long time many thought that Marco Polo introduced pasta to Italy following his expeditions to China, yet the earliest known reference to pasta in Italy predates the great explorer's return from China. Although Polo likely didn't introduce any-thing new to the Italians with his Chinese noodles, from that time on the consumption of pasta became increasingly popular. And it didn't take very long for Italian settlers to introduce their favorite food around the world, in European countries, North and South America, Africa and Australia.

Varieties of Pasta . . . .

People around the world have eaten traditional premade semoli-na pasta all their lives. Semolina is a pale flour made by milling durum wheat. Traditional pasta is made of white, refined flour with most of the important nutrients including the B-complex vitamins and all fiber removed. Consequently the flavor of the

People around the world have eaten traditional wheat pasta all their lives. Choose the whole-wheat variety for richer taste and better health.

pasta is bland. Lately, a variety of natural whole foods pastas have found their way into the marketplace. Not only do these pastas taste richer, they are also healthier in many different ways.

Spelt

Spelt is a grain that originated in Europe between five thousand and nine thousand years ago. Unlike many other grains, spelt has not been over-hybridized, genetically engineered and stripped of its flavor and nutrients. The taste of spelt pasta is similar to that of whole-wheat pasta but has a fuller and richer flavor. It is considered the most easily digested grain: spelt is highly water soluble, so nutrients can easily be absorbed by your body. People who have allergies to wheat can enjoy any spelt pasta dish without fear of a reaction.

Spelt contains valuable minerals and special carbohydrates that are important for blood clotting and stimulating the immune system. It is also an excellent source of crude fiber, which helps lower cholesterol levels, and contains more vitamins B_1 and B_2 than any other grains, as well as a substance called "anti-neoplastic vitamin B_{17}," which supports the body's cancer-fighting system. Finally, it is a "balanced" protein containing all of the eight essential amino acids your body requires. ("Essential" means your body cannot produce them and therefore you must get them from food).

Spelt contains a little more gluten than wheat, so if you

want to make your own spelt pasta, you must adjust the liquid-to-dry ingredient ratio. Start by using only three-quarters of the liquid required, then add more liquid, a little at a time, if necessary.

Kamut®

Kamut® is an ancient relative of modern durum wheat and has its origins in the fertile crescent of the Nile. "Kamut" is an ancient Egyptian word for wheat and means "Soul of the Earth."

It has a rich, buttery flavor and is easily digestible. Besides its higher profile of amino acids, vitamins, minerals and lipids (fats), Kamut® has 20 to 40 percent more protein than your average semolina noodles.

Kamut® makes outstanding pasta. It is superior to all other whole-grain pastas in texture and flavor. Kamut® provides more energy than other wheat, it is higher in eight of nine minerals, and contains up to 65 percent more amino acids. Its high percentage of lipids produces more energy in the body than carbohydrate. For this reason, Kamut® can be described as a "high energy grain."

Those who are allergic to wheat should try Kamut® pasta.

Amaranth

Its flavor is wild and woodsy and it has remarkable energizing qualities.

As early as 3,000 BC the Aztecs grew corn, beans, chili peppers and amaranth in the semi-arid Tehuacan valley of central Mexico. Amaranth was their staple and it was commonly known as "the grain of the gods." It is high in the essential amino acids lysine, methionine and cysteine. Amaranth is a better source of dietary fiber, calcium and iron than wheat pasta and its overall protein value — averaging over 16 percent — is higher than other foods including milk, soybeans, barley, wheat, peanuts and corn.

The Aztecs called amaranth "the grain of the gods."

Quinoa

The Incas in the Peruvian mountains centuries ago considered this grain so important that they called it quinoa, or "mother grain."

All grains are good for our health, but quinoa (pronounced "keen-wa") stands out as one of the most nutrient-rich grains. It contains more protein than any other grain and it is such a rich, balanced source of essential nutrients that it has been called the supergrain for the future!

Quinoa stands out as one of the most nutrient-rich grains.

Quinoa can wake you up! Most grains have only a little iron. Not quinoa — it is a very good source of iron, which your body needs to carry oxygen. Without iron, your red blood cells cannot function properly, and as a result the amount of oxygen carried to your cells is reduced. Heart and lungs then have to work harder and that causes fatigue over time. The magnesium and riboflavin in quinoa also help blood work more efficiently (half a cup of quinoa contains 90 milligrams of magnesium). Quinoa is also high in B vitamins, fiber, calcium and phosphorus and provides all essential amino acids, making it an important food especially for vegetarians since most plant sources rarely provide all these nutrients in such large amounts.

Pasta – Not Without Cheese!

Italy is a very cheesy country. It is said to produce as many as 451 different cheeses. I won't attempt to describe all of them here, but I will say a few words about the king of Italian cheese – Parmigiano.

The Story of Parmigiano

Parmesan, or Parmigiano as the Italians say, belongs to the family of the *formaggio grana* (grainy cheese). Grana is a hard cheese that is cooked but not pressed. One pound (a half kilogram) of Parmesan cheese is made with a little over seven quarts (seven liters) of the fresh, raw milk of cows that are fed only grass or hay. No artificial ingredients or high temperature are allowed to interfere with the natural aging process. The only other ingredients permitted are natural whey culture, rennet and salt, and then the cheese is aged for an average of two years.

Parmigiana Reggiano is produced in the Italian provinces of Parma, Mantua, Reggio Emilia, Modena, Bologna and the plains of the river Po. Parmigiana Reggiano is a whole food and has a

The formula for the king of Italian cheese, Parmesan, has remained unchanged over the last 800 years.

flavor that is unmistakably Old World. It is the so-called "great cheese of eight centuries"– its formula has remained unchanged over the last 800 years. This means that today's cheese is the same as that enjoyed by armored knights of the middle ages, bonded serfs, Renaissance masters, popes, kings and saints.

Pediatricians advise mothers and nurses to enrich baby food with Parmesan cheese. The proteins, fats, calcium, phosphorus and other vitamins and minerals in the cheese provide perfect nutrition for the baby during the first year of growth.

Use the Best Oils for Best Results

The body needs fat. However, your choice of fat deserves careful consideration – some fats will provide you with essential nutrients, and other fats will harm you.

Saturated fats are commonly derived from animals and from tropical oils such as coconut and palm. Saturated fats are solid at room temperature, are heat stable and suitable for frying. The body needs these fats for energy and any excess fat is stored for future use. Other than providing energy they have little nutritional value.

Unsaturated fats are divided into two groups, mono-unsaturated and poly-unsaturated fats. Mono-unsaturated oils are stable at room temperature and can be used for baking, sautéing and cooking, but not for deep frying, as they are heat stable only up to 223°F (106°C). Olive oil and avocado oil are mono-unsaturated.

Poly-unsaturated fats come from the oil of seeds. Most are liquid even when refrigerated and they quickly turn rancid when exposed to oxygen. Seed oils often contain good amounts of essential fatty acids, linolenic (omega-3) and linoleic (omega-6) fatty acids. These healthy fats can be found in significant proportions in flax, sunflower and pumpkin oil, but only if these oils are cold pressed and unrefined. They cannot be heated and should only be used in cold dishes and salads, or stirred into warm dishes. To give pasta a special flavor, toss cooked, warm pasta in the oil of your choice (for instance, unrefined walnut, hazelnut or pumpkin oil) before you add the actual sauce. The pasta will taste great – and better yet, it will be healthy!

The essential omega-3 and omega-6 fatty acids are the precursors of prostaglandins, hormone-like substances that play a key role in the normal function of the brain, skin, nervous system and sexual organs. Prostaglandins normalize cholesterol levels and protect against arteriosclerosis, cardiovascular disease and certain cancers.

Unfortunately, most supermarket oils are refined. The refining process not only removes taste and color, but also changes the heat-sensitive essential fatty acids (omega-3 and omega-6) into health-damaging trans-fatty acids. Likewise, the process called hydrogenation, which artificially hardens oil using high heat, turns healthy oil into unhealthy fats containing trans-fatty acids. Trans-fatty acids are not metabolized properly by the body and are linked to elevated cholesterol levels and the risk of cardiovascular disease. For your good health, avoid consuming trans-fatty acids – they are found in margarine, vegetable shortening and refined oils as well as hidden in commercially baked goods, salad dressings and fast foods. Good tasting, unrefined oils can be found in health food stores everywhere.

Butter is actually one of the healthiest fats for human consumption. Butter consists of saturated, mono- and poly-unsaturated fatty acids, and is easily absorbed by the body. As all other natural fats and unrefined oils, you can use butter to enhance the flavor of any dish.

A selection of natural, whole-grain pastas is finding its way into the marketplace, allowing for an unlimited variety of delicious pasta dishes.

Oils that should not be heated	Oils that can be lightly sautéed at low temperature	Oils that are safe when fried
Flax oil	Olive oil	Butter
Walnut oil	Hazelnut oil	Clarified butter (ghee)
Pumpkin oil	Sesame oil	Coconut oil and butter
Sunflower oil	Almond oil	Palm oil

Delicious Pasta

Recipes

Fettuccine with Roasted Pepper Pesto

This dish is perfect for a light summer lunch or dinner. The fettuccine complements the sweet bell pepper pesto better than any other pasta shape. Believe me – I have tried this pesto with many kinds of pasta but always I come back to fettuccine. The broad, flat surface of the noodle holds the sauce so you get the maximum amount of flavor in each bite.

7 oz (200 g) **fettuccine**

4 tbsp extra-virgin olive oil

2 cloves garlic, minced

1 medium shallot, minced

1 red bell pepper, julienned

1 yellow bell pepper, julienned

1 red onion, julienned

¼ cup (60 ml) **dry white wine**

¼ cup (60 ml) **cream**

1 tsp fresh thyme leaves

½ cup (125 ml) **Roasted Pepper Pesto** (see recipe page 59)

Sea salt and freshly ground pepper

Fresh Parmesan cheese

Cook the pasta in a large pot of boiling salted water; set aside.

Heat the oil in a large saucepan and sauté the garlic and shallot until soft. Add the peppers and onion and sauté for 2 to 3 minutes. Add the wine, cream, thyme and season with salt and pepper. Mix thoroughly. Add pesto and cook for 3 minutes. Add pasta and mix thoroughly. Garnish with shaved Parmesan. Serve immediately.

Serves 2

Tips for Cooking Perfect Pasta

- Always cook pasta in a large pot with plenty of water. This will help prevent the noodles from sticking together or adhering to the bottom of the pot.
Use the following table as a guide.

Pasta	Water	Salt
4–6 oz (125–175 g)	2 qt (2 l)	1 teaspoon
8–10 oz (250–300 g)	3 qt (3 l)	1½ teaspoons
12–14 oz (350–400 g)	4 qt (4 l)	2 teaspoons

- Make sure the water is boiling before you add the salt. Then allow the water to boil for two minutes before adding the pasta so that the salt has completely dissolved. Pasta cooked in salted water will taste better than pasta cooked in unsalted water.
- Add pasta to rapidly boiling water and stir gently to prevent the noodles from sticking to the pot.
- Close the lid in order to get the water boiling again.
- Taste the pasta from time to time until it is al dente, which means "firm to the bite." If your pasta is mushy or sticky it is overcooked; it will be difficult to serve and will taste starchy. For this reason alone it is important to test the pasta frequently while it is still in the pot.
- Always drain your pasta thoroughly; if too much water remains on the pasta (as can easily happen with shells, rigatoni and other hollow noodles) the sauce will separate from the noodles.

Fettuccine with Grilled Apple and Goat Cheese

I discovered the remarkable flavor combination of apples and goat's milk cheese when I was a boy. My family had a huge fruit orchard as well as a pasture for some goats. One morning I was coming in from the garden with a container of fresh goat's milk and I pulled an apple off the tree, which I ate and washed down with some goat's milk. I will never forget that taste! This dish brings these flavors together for anyone who has never had goats or an orchard in the back yard.

7 oz (200 g) fettuccine

I medium apple (choose a crunchy sort)

I½ qt (1⅘ l) water

I tbsp lemon

I bay leaf

2 cloves

6 tbsp extra-virgin olive oil

I tbsp butter

2 small shallots, finely chopped

I¾ oz (50 g or 10–12 pieces) sun-dried tomatoes

I tbsp fresh thyme, finely chopped

¼ cup (60 ml) apple cider

Sea salt, freshly ground pepper and nutmeg for seasoning

I¾ oz (50 g) goat's milk cheese, cut in chunks

Small branches of thyme for decoration

Peel the apple, cut it into broad slices ¼" (4 mm) thick and remove the seeds. Marinate the apple in the water, lemon, bay leaf and cloves for ½ hour.

Cook the fettuccine in a large pot of boiling salted water; set aside.

Take the apple slices out of the marinade, drain them and brush them with oil. Heat the apples in a saucepan, turning once so that the slices are golden brown on each side. An even better method is to grill them, if possible. Transfer them to a clean plate and set aside.

In the same pan in which you sautéed the apples, melt the butter and sauté the shallots, sun-dried tomatoes, thyme and the apple, and then add the apple cider. Season with pepper, salt and a pinch of nutmeg. Finally, add the noodles, and mix thoroughly. Serve on warm plates, top with a few chunks of goat cheese and decorate each serving with the thyme branches.

Serves 2

fettuccine

Tomato-Basil Spaghettini with Fennel

I cannot think of any other food that is at once as refreshing and healthy as fennel. Shaved thin, raw fennel livens up any salad; in pasta it gives a refreshing taste that combines very well with sour cream and lemon juice. Fennel is also widely known to improve blood circulation and is good for the digestive system.

Cook the spaghettini in a large pot of boiling salted water; set aside.

In a large saucepan heat the butter and oil together (this prevents the butter from burning). Add the garlic and sauté for one minute then add the other vegetables and sauté for 3 to 4 minutes or until they are tender. Add the wine and lemon juice, turn the heat to high and boil for 2 minutes. Add the sour cream, cream and tarragon. Season with salt and pepper then turn the heat to medium and reduce the sauce by half. Add the pasta and mix thoroughly. Serve on warm plates and garnish with a few fennel fronds.

Serves 2

7 oz (200 g) tomato-basil spaghettini

1 tbsp butter

3–4 tbsp extra-virgin olive oil

2–3 cloves garlic, finely chopped

1 small red onion, julienned

1 small fennel bulb, julienned (keep the feathery fronds for garnish)

1 stalk celery, julienned

1 small zucchini, julienned

¼ cup (60 ml) dry white wine

2 tbsp fresh lemon juice

3 tbsp sour cream

½ cup (125 ml) cream

1 tbsp fresh tarragon, finely chopped

Sea salt and freshly ground pepper

spaghettini

Tomato spaghettini gets its color from tomato paste. You can make your own fresh tomato spaghettini by adding tomato paste to your dough.

Pasta Bonbons

My mother has a saying that goes: "The longer food takes to make, the longer the taste will stay in your mouth." This certainly applies to these unique bundles which reward you for the extra effort needed to prepare them. Once you have made *Pasta Bonbons*, you will never eat any of the individual ingredients again without thinking of this recipe. For a main course serve twelve bonbons per person; for an appetizer serve six bonbons per person.

Filling

2 butternut squash (1–1½ lbs each or 450–675 g)

2 tbsp butter

1 cup (300 g) small amaretto cookies, crushed

2 tbsp ground hazelnuts or walnuts

1 tbsp sage, minced

½ cup (300 g) freshly grated asagio cheese

Sea salt and freshly ground pepper

1 package won ton wraps (at least 12 individual wraps), 3" (8 cm) square

Sauce

½ cup (125 ml) dry white wine

2 tbsp sun-dried red currants (or cranberries)

½ cup (125 ml) cream

½ tsp saffron

Sea salt & freshly ground pepper

Preheat the oven to 450°F (225°C).

Cut the butternut squash in half and remove the seeds. Cut butter in chunks and place an even amount on each of the open squash halves. Cover the squash with foil and bake for 30 to 35 minutes.

In a small bowl combine the amaretto cookies, nuts, sage and cheese.

Take the squash out of the oven and let it cool. Remove the peel with a spoon and set the squash in a very fine sieve and allow the liquid to drain. After the liquid has completely gone, season the squash with pepper and salt, mix it with the other ingredients and refrigerate for about 5 minutes.

Lay two won ton leaves next to each other, brush the edge with a wet pastry brush and overlapping their edges slightly. Put 1½ tsp of the filling in the middle of the won ton leaves. Wrap the filling in the leaves and twist the ends of the leaves like a candy wrapper.

Lay a clean kitchen cloth on a plate, set each bonbon on top and refrigerate for at least an hour. This step can be completed up to a day in advance.

In a large saucepan, heat the wine and currants and bring to a boil. Add the cream and saffron, stir gently and let the sauce reduce by ⅔ (the consistency should be like melted butter). Put the bonbons in a large pot of boiling water and cook for 3 minutes. Remove the bonbons from the water, drain, arrange them on a warm plate and pour the sauce over top.

Makes 24 to 30 bonbons

Farfalle with Walnuts and Gorgonzola Cheese

Walnuts and blue cheese is a flavor combination that is as old as "salt and pepper." In this recipe I use Gorgonzola, which is a type of blue cheese but does not have such a strong "blue cheese" flavor. It has a pleasant creamy taste and complements the walnuts and spinach better than any other type of blue cheese. This dish is very easy to make and very easy to eat!

7 oz (200 g) farfalle (bowties)

I tsp minced garlic

I tbsp butter

I½ tbsp crushed walnuts (or more to taste)

I cup (250 ml) cream

I tbsp Gorgonzola (or blue cheese)

Sea salt, freshly ground pepper and nutmeg

I cup (I bunch) **fresh spinach leaves**

Freshly grated Parmesan cheese

Cook the farfalle in a large pot of boiling salted water; set aside.

In a large saucepan, sauté the garlic in the butter until golden. Add the walnuts, cream and cheese and heat through until the cheese has melted and blended with the cream. Season with salt, pepper and nutmeg. Add the farfalle and spinach to the sauce and toss. Serve immediately with freshly grated Parmesan.

Serves 2

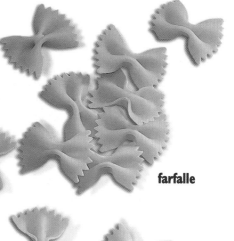

farfalle

The spinach should be added immediately before serving. This maintains its color and prevents it from overcooking.

Rigatoni Arrabiata

I did not invent this recipe. You can find it anywhere in the south of Italy where the hot weather invites spicy foods. The "heat" in the sauce (*arrabiata* is Italian for "hot and spicy") actually cools your body down; the salt from the olives and capers will restore sodium to your system. If you like your pasta really hot, add more chili flakes.

7 oz (200 g) rigatoni

2 medium shallots, minced

1 tsp garlic, minced

3 tbsp extra-virgin olive oil

2 tbsp pitted Kalamata olives

1 tbsp capers (optional)

⅔ cup (160 ml) Basic Tomato Sauce (see recipe page 61)

2 tsp fresh herbs such as thyme, rosemary and oregano

1 tsp chili flakes (or more if you like it spicy)

Sea salt and freshly ground pepper

1 tbsp butter

Freshly grated Parmesan cheese

Fresh basil leaves for garnish

Cook the rigatoni in a large pot of boiling salted water; set aside.

In a large saucepan, sauté the shallots and garlic in the olive oil. Do not let the garlic burn. Add the olives and capers and sauté for 3 minutes longer. Add the tomato sauce and blend. Add herbs, chili flakes, salt and pepper and mix thoroughly. Next, add the butter to the sauce and let it melt. Finally, add the pasta and toss.

Garnish with freshly grated Parmesan and basil leaves and serve.

Serves 2

rigatoni

If you do not want to use wine for cooking, substitute an equal amount of the pasta water before you pour it away but make sure that it is not too salty.

Mediterranean Pasta

This dish is so full of vitamins (especially vitamins A, B and C), fiber and carbohydrates that if you sat in a boat after eating it, you would be able to paddle to the end of the ocean with energy to spare! This meal is also very easy to digest and is perfect for a warm weather dinner.

7 oz (200 g) penne

1 small zucchini

1 red bell pepper

1 yellow bell pepper

1 eggplant

1 Belgian endive

¼ cup (150 g) pitted Kalamata olives (pit your own; avoid canned olives)

Sea salt and freshly ground pepper

6 tbsp extra-virgin olive oil

5–6 cloves garlic, minced

1 medium shallot, minced

½ cup cherry tomatoes, cut in half

½ cup (125 ml) dry white wine

3½ oz (100 g) feta cheese

1 tbsp each of minced fresh basil, rosemary, thyme and oregano

Cook pasta in a large pot of boiling salted water; set aside.

Wash and slice vegetables, season with salt and pepper and 2 tbsp olive oil. Grill vegetables until tender then set aside, or roast them in the oven if you don't have a grill.

In the meantime, sauté the garlic and shallot in 4 tbsp olive oil. Add tomatoes, white wine, and cook for 4 to 5 minutes over high heat. Add the pasta and feta cheese and mix thoroughly, then add the herbs and toss again.

Place grilled vegetables on top of the pasta and serve.

Serves 2

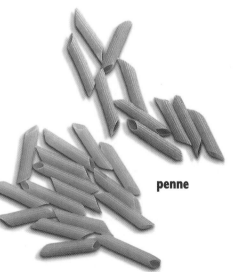

penne

Farfalle with Orange

The orange is a fascinating fruit that is not often paired with pasta. If someone would have told me as a boy to eat an orange with my pasta, I would have said they were out of their mind! But you never know the taste until you try it. This is a great summer dish that can also be served cold.

7 oz (200 g) farfalle

½ cup (100 g) snowpeas

1 medium shallot, minced

4 tbsp butter

½ cup (125 ml) freshly squeezed orange juice

1 cup (250 ml) cream

Freshly ground pepper

Orange segments from one orange, all rind and pith removed

10 cumquats, halved but not peeled

1 tsp fresh thyme leaves or rosemary for garnish

Cook pasta in a large pot of boiling salted water; set aside.

Cook the snowpeas in 1 quart (1 liter) of boiling water for 2 minutes then drain and rinse immediately with ice cold water.

Gently sauté the shallot in 1 tbsp butter. Add the orange juice, cream and cumquats and cook on high for 2 to 3 minutes. Add the rest of the butter to the sauce and season with pepper. Finally, add the pasta, snow peas and orange segments and mix thoroughly.

Garnish with fresh thyme and serve.

Serves 2

faralle

Curried Rotini Salad with Pineapple

This salad can be made up ahead of time and chilled, if desired. I invented this dish because an East Indian friend who never had the patience to cook wanted to have something nourishing on hand whenever hunger struck. With this salad he would just open the fridge door and enjoy the rich flavors of his homeland.

7 oz (200 g) rotini

1 lb (450 g) broccoli, stems removed

½ red onion, julienned

2 green onions, chopped

1 red bell pepper, cut in ¼" pieces

1 tbsp fresh tarragon, chopped

½ cup (150 g) fresh pineapple, diced

⅔ cup (160 ml) cream

⅔ cup (160 ml) coconut milk

1 tsp cracked chili

1 tbsp brown sugar

1 tbsp curry powder

Cook pasta in a large pot of boiling salted water; set aside.

Steam the broccoli 3 to 4 minutes. In a warm saucepan, add the cream, coconut milk, curry powder, sugar and reduce until curry powder and sugar dissolve. Add salt and pepper to taste. Add the chili flakes then let sauce simmer until it has reduced to ½ cup. Set aside and let cool slightly.

In a large mixing bowl, add onions (green and red), broccoli, pineapple, pasta, tarragon and mix thoroughly. Pour the curry cream over top and mix thoroughly again. Allow to sit for 10 minutes before serving so that the flavors can incorporate.

Serves 2

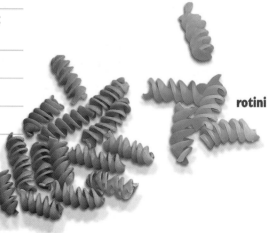

rotini

Do not pour the sauce over the ingredients while it is hot or if it is too cold. The sauce is best added when it feels slightly warm to the touch.

Shells and Broccoli

George Bush, ex-President of the United States, is probably the only person who would not like this dish. I used to serve this at my first restaurant and ninety percent of the people who tried it wanted to take the recipe home. Good pasta hardly gets any simpler than this.

7 oz (200 g) **pasta shells**

1½ lbs (680 g) **broccoli**

½ cup (125 ml) **extra-virgin olive oil**

4 cloves garlic, minced

¼ cup (150 g) **Kalamata olives**

¾ cup (250 g) **fresh plum tomatoes, cut into chunks**

1 tsp fresh oregano

1 tsp chili flakes

½ cup (125 ml) **dry white wine**

1 tbsp Basil Pesto (see recipe page 60)

2 tbsp butter

Freshly grated Parmesan cheese

Cook pasta shells in a large pot of boiling salted water; set aside.

Trim and cook the broccoli in 2 quarts (2 liters) of boiling salted water for 3 minutes then drain and rinse with cold water.

Heat the oil in a large saucepan then add the garlic, olives, tomatoes, oregano, chili flakes and finally the broccoli and basil pesto. Mix thoroughly. Add the wine then turn the heat to high and boil for 2 minutes. Add the pasta and butter; mix thoroughly and serve with freshly grated Parmesan.

Serves 2

pasta shells

Mezza Luna with Arugula, Pine Nuts and Ricotta Cheese

For this recipe you can use fresh homemade pasta or round won ton wraps, which are easier to use.

1½ lbs (680 g) **arugula**

4 cloves **garlic**

1 medium **shallot**

½ cup (200 g) **ricotta cheese**

Sea salt, freshly ground pepper and ground nutmeg

4 tbsp **pine nuts, roasted**

¼ cup (150 g) **breadcrumbs**

¼ cup (150 g) **freshly grated Parmesan cheese**

1 full recipe of **Homemade Pasta** (see page 58) **or 16 sheets of round won ton wraps.**

¼ cup (60 ml) **Basic Tomato Sauce** (see page 61)

¼ cup (170 g) **fresh tomatoes, diced**

¼ cup (125 ml) **cream**

36

At least an hour ahead of time, place the ricotta cheese in some cheesecloth or a colander and drain until there is no liquid left.

Wash and dry the arugula and separate 1 handful for later use. Place the garlic, shallot and arugula in a food processor and pulse 4 or 5 times. Add the ricotta a bit at a time while the food processor is running. Season with salt, pepper and nutmeg. Add the pine nuts and process for 1 to 2 minutes or until the mixture turns into a thick paste. Put this mixture in a large bowl and add breadcrumbs and Parmesan cheese and mix thoroughly. Adjust seasoning if necessary.

If you are using homemade pasta, roll it into thin sheets then cut 16 circles 3" (7.5 cm) in diameter. (Roll trimmings back into a ball, wrap and return to refrigerator.) If you are using won ton wraps, lay them out on a dry surface. Place one teaspoon of filling in the middle of each circle and brush the edge of the circle with a wet pastry brush. Fold the circle in a half-moon shape and press the edges together.

Bring a large pot of salted water to boil. In the meantime, heat the tomato sauce, fresh tomatoes and cream in a large saucepan over high heat and reduce by half.

In the meantime, drop the mezza lunas into the boiling water and cook for 3 to 4 minutes or until they float to the surface.

Add the remaining arugula to the sauce, reduce heat to minimum and cook for 1 minute.

Scoop out the mezza lunas and drain thoroughly, set on warm plates and pour the sauce over top. Serve with shaved Parmesan cheese.

Serves 2

Linguine with Bell Peppers and Cream Cheese Sauce

Dijon mustard and cream cheese taste wonderful together and they make an excellent foundation for a pasta sauce. This is a very refreshing dish.

7 oz (200 g) **linguine**

1 medium **red, yellow and green pepper**

1 medium **white onion**

1 small **zucchini**

3 cloves **garlic, sliced**

3 tbsp **extra-virgin olive oil**

½ cup (125 ml) **dry white wine**

7 oz (200 g) **cream cheese, cubed**

¼ cup (60 ml) **cream**

1 tbsp **Dijon mustard**

Sea salt, freshly ground pepper and nutmeg

1 tbsp **Italian parsley, chopped**

Cook the linguine in a large pot of boiling salted water; set aside.

Cut the peppers, onion and zucchini in ½" (1 cm) pieces. Sauté the onion, garlic, peppers and zucchini in the olive oil for 2 minutes. Do not overcook the vegetables. Add white wine and the cream cheese and stir with a wooden spoon until the cheese dissolves in the wine. Don't worry if the cheese curdles; the sauce will become smooth later in the cooking process. Add the cream and mustard and stir until all ingredients are incorporated. Season to taste with salt, pepper and nutmeg and reduce sauce by half. Add the pasta and parsley; mix thoroughly and serve.

Serves 2

linguine

Gemelli with Root Vegetables

When I start making this dish my friends stand in the kitchen with forks in their hands, ready to eat. Believe me, you can make a lot of friends with this dish!

7 oz (200 g) gemelli

⅔ cup (150 g) rutabaga

⅔ cup (150 g) carrots

⅔ cup (100 g) parsnips

⅔ cup (100 g) asparagus

½ cup (150 g) celery root or stalk

4 tbsp extra-virgin olive oil

¼ cup red onion, julienned

4 cloves garlic

⅔ cup (160 ml) Marsala wine (or vin santo or sweet sherry)

2 tbsp butter

1 tsp each fresh Italian parsley, thyme and rosemary, finely chopped

Sea salt and freshly ground pepper

Peel and slice all vegetables into 1½" (3.5 cm) segments.

Cook pasta in a large pot of boiling salted water; set aside.

Bring 2 quarts (2 liters) of salted water to boil in a medium pot and cook all vegetables except the red onion and garlic for 5 to 6 minutes; drain and set aside.

Heat the oil in a large saucepan and sauté the onion and garlic until golden brown. Add the other vegetables and mix thoroughly. Add the Marsala and cook for 4 to 5 minutes on high or until the Marsala has reduced by half. Add the butter, herbs and salt and pepper to taste. Finally add the pasta, mix thoroughly and serve.

Serves 2

gemelli

Risoni Salad with Broccoli

This delicious, hearty and healthy salad is a great party dish. It has so many wonderful ingredients that there is something to please everybody. It is great for the cook, too, as it can be prepared ahead of time and be ready to serve when the hunger hits!

7 oz (200 g) **risoni** (orzo)

I cup (300 g) **broccoli florets**

10 fresh baby corns, sliced in ¼" (5 mm) lengths (or you can use canned baby corn if fresh ones aren't available)

I medium carrot, julienned

I medium red onion, julienned

½ small cucumber

I tbsp each freshly chopped thyme, oregano and lavender, if available, otherwise use fresh rosemary

½ cup (125 ml) **balsamic vinegar**

½ cup (125 ml) **extra-virgin olive oil**

I tbsp freshly squeezed lemon juice

Sea salt and freshly ground pepper

Cook risoni in a large pot of boiling salted water; set aside.

Cook the broccoli and fresh baby corn in a large pot of boiling salted water for 3 minutes; drain and rinse immediately with cold water. This maintains the bright color of the vegetables after cooking.

Cut the cucumber in half lengthwise, remove the seeds and then cut into ¼" (5 mm) pieces.

In a large mixing bowl, add all the vegetables, herbs, balsamic vinegar, olive oil and lemon juice and mix thoroughly. Add the risoni last and mix thoroughly again. Season with salt and pepper and serve.

Serves 2

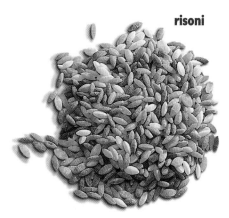

risoni

The reason the risoni is added last is so that the vegetables have a chance to take on the flavor of the dressing. Otherwise the risoni would absorb all the dressing.

Open-Faced Lasagne with Tomato Confit

This unusual lasagne has several advantages over traditional lasagne. First, the flavor of each individual ingredient is more prominent; it is easier and quicker to make than traditional lasagne; the impressive look of the vegetable tower is an unusual and attractive presentation; ingredients such as tomato confit, goat cheese and arugula are used, which are not often found in traditional lasagnes.

I large beefsteak tomato, cut in ½" (1 cm) **slices**

I medium eggplant, cut in ½" (1 cm) **slices**

I yellow bell pepper, cut in 4 segments

2 portobellini mushrooms (or I portobello mushroom or I oyster mushroom), stems removed

I tsp garlic, minced

I medium red onion, cut in ½" (1 cm) **slices**

¼ cup (60 ml) **plus 2 tbsp extra-virgin olive oil**

Sea salt and freshly ground pepper

8 sheets of lasagne noodles

I lb (450 g) **arugula** (or spinach)

I tbsp butter

3½ oz (100 g) **goat cheese**

I cup (250 ml) **Tomato Confit** (see recipe page 61)

¼ cup (150 g) **fresh basil leaves**

Preheat oven to 425°F (225°C). Place all vegetables except the arugula in a large bowl with ¼ cup olive oil. Mix thoroughly and season with salt and pepper. Lay the vegetables on a cookie sheet and roast them in the oven for 7 to 10 minutes. Keep the oven on, you will need to use it again to heat the vegetable tower immediately before serving.

In the meantime, cook the lasagne sheets in a large pot of boiling salted water. Drain and set aside the noodles but save the water. Simmer the water on low, as you will need it to heat the noodles immediately before serving.

Sauté the arugula in the remaining olive oil and the butter for 2 minutes or until soft.

The next step involves forming 2 towers using the vegetables. Note that you must place two basil leaves between each layer. On a clean cookie tray or an ovenproof plate, start each vegetable tower with 1 tomato slice, followed by 1 eggplant slice, 1 onion slice, 1 bell pepper segment, 1 portobellini mushroom, ½ of the arugula, ½ the goat cheese and finally 2 tbsp of the tomato confit. Don't forget to place 2 basil leaves between each layer. Place the tray in the oven and bake for 3 to 4 minutes.

In the meantime, plunge the lasagne sheets back into the boiling water and heat through for 1 or 2 minutes. Drain the noodles thoroughly and arrange 4 sheets decoratively on each plate (see photo). Place the remaining tomato confit on the lasagne sheets. Set the vegetable tower in the middle and serve.

Serves 2

Rotini Picante

Once I invited to my house two friends who had never before met each other. One came from Italy, the other from India. They were hungry and each asked me to cook them something special that would remind them of home. I invented this dish on the spot and they were so happy I felt like a successful diplomat! This dish is great for company.

7 oz (200 g) rotini

¼ cup (60 ml) extra-virgin olive oil

4 cloves garlic, sliced

2 medium shallots, sliced

¼ cup (150 g) diced tomatoes

1 medium carrot, julienned

1 small red bell pepper, julienned

1 small yellow bell pepper, julienned

1 medium zucchini, julienned

2 tbsp green onions, chopped

¼ cup (100 g) fresh peas (or frozen if fresh are not available)

¼ cup (100 g) mushrooms, sliced

¼ cup (60 ml) white wine (or pasta water only if wine is not available)

1½ tsp curry powder

Cook the rotini in a large pot of boiling salted water; set aside.

Heat the oil in a large saucepan and sauté the garlic and shallot for 1 to 2 minutes. Add the remaining vegetables and sauté for 2 minutes. Then add the white wine, curry powder and herbs and cook for another 2 minutes. Add the tomato sauce and reduce the sauce by half. Add the butter and season to taste with salt and pepper. Add the pasta and mix thoroughly. Garnish with freshly grated (or shaved) Parmesan or pecorino and serve.

Serves 2

2 tsp fresh or dried herbs of any kind

½ cup (125 ml) Basic Tomato Sauce (see recipe page 61)

1 tbsp butter

Sea salt and freshly ground pepper

Freshly grated Parmesan or pecorino cheese

rotini

Sicilian Style Pasta

My Sicilian friend once said the best pasta sauces come from Sicily. I thought he was exaggerating until I tried this sauce. The combination of salted ricotta with grilled eggplant, fresh tomatoes and basil left me gasping for more. This is a very easy dish to make as long as you have some *Basil Pesto* and *Basic Tomato Sauce* on hand. See pages 60 and 61 for recipes.

7 oz (200 g) **penne**

1 medium eggplant

¼ cup (60 ml) **extra-virgin olive oil**

4 cloves garlic, minced

1 medium shallot, minced

2 tbsp Basil Pesto (see recipe page 60)

¼ cup (60 ml) **dry white wine**

½ cup (125 ml) **Basic Tomato Sauce** (see recipe page 61)

1 cup (300 g) **cherry tomatoes, cut in half**

Freshly chopped herbs (basil, thyme and oregano work well but you can use any herbs to suit your own taste)

½ cup (100 g) **freshly grated salted ricotta**

Freshly ground pepper to taste

Preheat the oven to 375°F (200°C).

Cook the penne in a large pot of boiling salted water; set aside.

Slice the eggplant into ½" (1 cm) slices, brush both sides with olive oil, lay them on a cookie sheet and roast in the oven until golden brown. Cut eggplant slices into cubes.

In a large saucepan, heat the remaining olive oil and sauté garlic, shallot, eggplant and pesto until the eggplant and shallots are soft. Add the wine and toss for a few seconds then add the tomato sauce, fresh tomatoes and herbs and reduce until the sauce has the consistency of a paste. Add the pasta and the ricotta cheese and mix thoroughly. Garnish with fresh herbs and serve.

Serves 2

If you would like to make your own salt-cured ricotta, empty a container of fresh ricotta onto a plate and sprinkle sea salt over the entire surface. Set in a cool place (not the refrigerator) and leave for three weeks.

During the first week you should drain the liquid daily and sprinkle more salt over the surface of the cheese. The sea salt will draw all of the moisture out of the cheese in this time and therefore it is necessary to keep applying salt until the ricotta is as hard as an apple.

You can even flavor your salt-cured ricotta (as I have done in the picture to the right) by sprinkling dry herbs, chili flakes or freshly ground pepper over the cheese before the initial application of salt. Do not break the cheese apart until the curing process is complete.

Home-made salt-cured ricotta will keep in the refrigerator for 3 to 4 months if kept in plastic wrap.

Orecchiette with Apricots, Red Peppercorns and Cashews

Orecchiette, or pig's ears, makes an unusual pasta dish that has a robust texture and a unique blend of flavors. The sauce is sweet and buttery and gets its freshness from the thyme.

7 oz (200 g) orecchiette (pig's ears)

½ cup (125 ml) dry white wine

I tbsp maple syrup or honey

½ cup (100 g) dried apricots

¼ cup (60 ml) raw cashews

2 tbsp extra-virgin olive oil

3 tbsp butter

I small red onion, minced

I tbsp fresh thyme leaves

I tbsp red peppercorns

Sea salt and freshly ground pepper

Asiago cheese

In a medium-size bowl, marinate the apricots in the wine and maple syrup (or honey) for 1 hour.

Cook the orecchiette in a large pot of boiling salted water; set aside.

In the meantime, dry roast the cashews in a hot skillet, tossing continually until they are a light gold color; set aside.

In a saucepan, heat the olive oil and 1 tbsp butter over low heat then add the onion and cook until soft. Add the apricots and the marinade, turn the heat to high and reduce the sauce by half (approximately 4 minutes). Add the cashews and pasta and mix thoroughly. Add the thyme and peppercorns and mix thoroughly again. Season to taste with salt and pepper and serve with shaved asiago cheese.

Serves 2

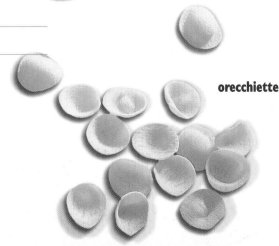

orecchiette

Pappardelle with Wild Mushrooms

The Marsala and mushrooms taste wonderful together and the entire dish can be made in no time. Pappardelle with wild mushrooms and a nice glass of wine is ample reward for a hard day at the office.

7 oz (200 g) **pappardelle**

½ lb (225 g) **shiitake mushrooms**

½ lb (225 g) **oyster mushrooms**

½ lb (225 g) **regular** (white) **mushrooms**

½ lb (225 g) **Chanterelle mushrooms** (or dried porcini mushrooms, soaked in warm water for 20 minutes; reserve soak water)

1 medium leek

4 tbsp extra-virgin olive oil

5 or 6 cloves garlic, minced

2 small shallots, minced

½ cup (125 ml) **Marsala wine** (or medium dry sherry)

½ cup (125 ml) **cream**

1 tbsp each fresh thyme, tarragon, rosemary and sage (or substitute 1 tbsp Basil Pesto – see recipe on page 60)

Freshly grated asiago cheese

Cook the pappardelle in a large pot of boiling salted water; set aside.

Cut the mushrooms and leek in ½" (1 cm) slices. For best effect, cut the leek diagonally.

Heat the oil in a large saucepan and sauté the garlic and shallots for 2 minutes. Add mushrooms and leek and sauté for 4 to 5 minutes. Add the Marsala (and if you have used porcini mushrooms, add 2 tbsp of the reserved soak liquid at this time). Cook for 3 minutes then add cream and fresh herbs. Reduce sauce by half. Add pasta and mix thoroughly. Garnish with asiago cheese and serve immediately.

Serves 2

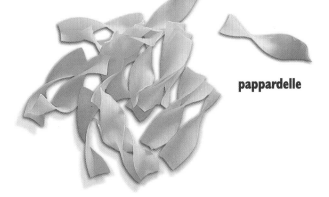

pappardelle

Do not wash Chanterelles as they will absorb too much water and lose some of their buttery, nutty taste. Instead, brush away any dirt with a clean, dry pastry brush.

Parmesan will overpower the delicate flavor of the mushrooms. Freshly grated asiago is the ideal cheese to serve with this dish.

Penne with Baby Bocconcini and Cherry Tomatoes

Researchers say you can never have enough tomatoes in your diet – and I agree! This dish is full of the flavor of fresh cherry tomatoes and is a light, easy-to-digest meal that is ready in no time.

7 oz (200 g) penne

¼ cup (60 ml) plus 3 tbsp extra-virgin olive oil

2 cloves garlic, minced

1 medium shallot, slivered (or 2 tbsp chopped green onion)

½ cup (125 ml) dry white wine

10–12 cherry tomatoes, cut in half

¼ cup (150 g) fresh basil, chopped

1 tbsp butter

Sea salt & freshly ground pepper

3.5 oz (100 g) baby bocconcini (roughly 6–8 balls), **cut in half**

1 tbsp balsamic vinegar

Cook penne in a large pot of boiling salted water; set aside.

Heat the oil in a saucepan and sauté the garlic and shallot until golden brown. Add the wine and reduce by half. Add the tomatoes, basil and butter, tossing gently. Season with salt and pepper.

Add the pasta and the bocconcini to the sauce and toss. Finally, add the balsamic vinegar and serve.

Serves 2

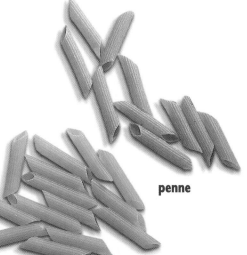

penne

This dish must be served immediately otherwise the bocconcini will stick together.

Beet-Pistachio Ravioli
with Paprika-Cream Sauce

Beets, sage, pistachios, asiago... . Each of these ingredients has a flavor and texture that combines very well with the others. This is a sure-fire crowd-pleaser.

Ravioli

1 lb (450 g) red beets

2 tbsp pistachio nuts, ground fine

½ cup (300 g) asiago cheese

½ tbsp fresh chopped sage

1 full portion of Homemade Pasta (see recipe page 58) **or lasagne sheets** (see note below)

Sea salt and freshly ground pepper

3 tbsp extra-virgin olive oil

2 cloves garlic, minced

1 medium shallot, diced

1 large tbsp sweet paprika

¼ cup (60 ml) dry white wine

⅔ cup (160 ml) cream

2 tsp maple syrup or honey

Cook the red beets until soft then rinse them under cold water. Peel the beets, cut them into chunks and pulse them in a food processor three or four times. Add the nuts, cheese and sage, season with salt and pepper and blend thoroughly in the food processor.

Using a pasta machine, roll out the pasta into thin sheets and cut into twelve 3" (7.5 cm) squares. Lay out the pasta squares and place one spoonful of the filling in the center of each square. Brush the edges of each pasta square with a wet (water) pastry brush then lay another square on top. Press all edges together using your fingers and pinch the squares together so that all the air comes out. Bring a large pot of salted water to boil.

In a large saucepan, heat the oil over medium heat and sauté the garlic and shallot until golden brown. Add the paprika and stir for 30 seconds then add the wine, cream and maple syrup. Reduce by half.

Drop the ravioli one by one into the boiling water (keep the flat side facing up) and stir gently to prevent the pasta from sticking to the bottom of the pot. Cook for 4 minutes. (If you are using lasagne sheets, cook for 5 minutes.) Drain thoroughly then place ravioli on serving plates and pour the sauce over top. Serve immediately.

Yields 6 large ravioli

If you are in a hurry, you can substitute homemade pasta with thin, flat lasagne sheets. Soak the sheets in a large amount of warm water until softened. Drain and pat dry with a clean dish towel. Cut to desired size and proceed with the recipe.

Homemade Pasta

Making homemade pasta is as easy as A B C. There are only three ingredients and a dough can be made in ten minutes and, if you like, it can be safely stored in the freezer until you need to use it.

7 oz (200 g) whole-grain flour

2 large eggs, at room temperature

2 tbsp extra-virgin olive oil or cold-pressed vegetable oil

Pour the flour in a mound on a clean, flat surface. Make a well in the middle of the mound and place the eggs and oil in the well. Using a wooden spoon, gently draw the flour into the well and mix it with the eggs. (If the eggs happen to run over the edge you can catch them with a pastry scraper.)

Once all ingredients are combined in a rough ball, take the dough in your hands and knead it until the surface is smooth.

Wrap the dough in plastic wrap and let it rest in the fridge for at least 15 minutes. Before you use the dough, take it out of the fridge and let it sit for 5 minutes. This will improve its elasticity.

You can make pasta dough well ahead of time and divide it into portions and freeze it. Remember to allow time to let the dough thaw before you work with it.

How To Make Ravioli

You will need to start with one full portion of *Homemade Pasta* (see recipe page 58). Using a pasta machine, roll out the pasta and cut into 3" (7.5 cm) strips. Place spoonfuls of filling onto the strips, leaving 3" (7.5 cm) between each spoonful. Cut out squares, making sure the filling is in the middle. Brush the edges of each pasta square with a wet (with water) pastry brush then lay another square on top. Press all edges together using your fingers and pinch the squares together so that all the air comes out.

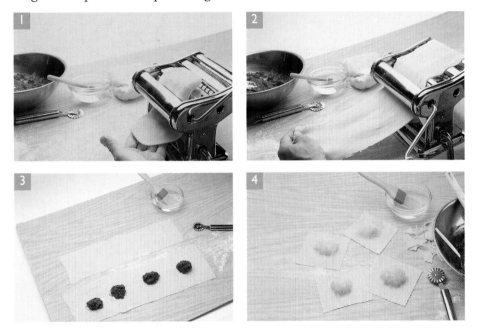

Arugula Pesto

2 lbs (1 kg) arugula

½ cup (250 g) Macadamia nuts (or any other type)

5 cloves garlic

dash white wine vinegar

¼ cup (150 g) Parmesan cheese, freshly grated

Wash the arugula and remove the stems. Pulse twice in food processor then add the nuts, garlic, vinegar, cheese and blend. Add the oil slowly while the machine is running and incorporate all ingredients. This should take about 5 minutes. Season to taste with salt and pepper.

⅔ cup (160 ml) cold-pressed sunflower oil or extra-virgin olive oil

Sea salt and freshly ground pepper

Basil Pesto

½ cup (250 g) **pine nuts**

3 lbs (1.3 kg) **fresh basil leaves**

¼ cup (120 g) **chopped garlic cloves**

1 cup (250 ml) **extra-virgin olive oil**

1 tbsp **sea salt**

1 tbsp **freshly ground pepper**

¼ cup (150 g) **finely grated Parmesan cheese**

Heat a cast-iron saucepan and roast the pine nuts until they are golden brown. Wash and dry the basil thoroughly then place in a food processor along with the garlic and pine nuts. Turn food processor on and slowly add olive oil until you get a thick, creamy sauce. Add the salt and pepper and blend again. Incorporate the Parmesan with a spoon (do not blend anymore).

Leftover basil pesto should be frozen.

Never cook fresh basil as it will turn black and taste bitter.

Sun-Dried Tomato Pesto

1 lb (450 g) **sun-dried tomatoes**

5 cloves **garlic**

2 dried **bay leaves**

2 tbsp **maple syrup**

⅔ cup (125 ml) **extra-virgin olive oil**

¼ cup (100 g) **roasted pecans or pine nuts**

2 tbsp **oregano** (or cilantro, tarragon, rosemary or basil – whatever you please)

¼ cup (150 g) **freshly grated Parmesan cheese**

Bring 2 quarts (2 liters) of water to a boil and add the tomatoes, 2 cloves of garlic, the bay leaves and the maple syrup (the maple syrup removes the acidity from the tomatoes). Cook on high heat for 1½ minutes – no more. Drain the water and rinse the ingredients with cold water; let cool.

Remove the bay leaves. Place the tomatoes and garlic and remaining ingredients in the food processor and pulse twice then slowly add the oil while the machine is running. Use your judgement when adding oil: the end result should not look like a paste; it should have a chunky consistency.

Put in a jar and refrigerate for up to 2 months.

Tomato Confit

- 8 medium-size beef steak tomatoes, halved and seeds removed
- ½ cup (120 ml) **extra-virgin olive oil**
- 10 cloves garlic, thinly sliced
- ½ tsp each freshly chopped rosemary, thyme, basil, sage and parsley
- 1 bunch or ¼ cup (100 g) chopped green onions
- ½ tsp freshly squeezed lime juice
- Sea salt and freshly ground pepper

Preheat oven to 500°F (250°C).

In a bowl, season tomato pieces with salt and pepper and mix with ¼ cup (60 ml) olive oil. Spread the pieces cut side down on a baking tray and bake on the highest level for 3 to 5 minutes. They are done when the skin shrinks. Remove from oven, set on a plate and let cool.

In the meantime, heat ¼ cup (60 ml) of olive oil in a saucepan, add the garlic and heat just until the garlic turns gold. Immediately remove the garlic from the oil and set aside.

Once the tomatoes have cooled, peel them and cut them into large pieces. Mix the garlic and the tomatoes and season with the herbs, onions, salt and pepper. Add the lime juice and serve.

Basic Tomato Sauce

Making a good tomato sauce is always a challenge. The balance of flavors in this sauce took years to refine and the result is a classic taste that can be used on its own or can be combined with recipes.

- ½ cup (125 ml) **extra-virgin olive oil**
- 1 medium onion, minced
- 4 cloves garlic, minced
- 1 tsp each dried oregano, basil, tarragon, marjoran and chili flakes
- ½ cup (125 ml) **dry white wine**
- 15 oz (500 ml) **crushed Italian plum tomatoes**
- ½ cup (125 ml) **of water**
- Sea salt
- 1 finely shredded carrot
- Fresh basil leaves for garnish

Heat olive oil in a large pot, add onion, garlic, herbs and chili flakes and sauté until the onions are golden brown. Add wine, tomatoes and water. Season with salt. Add carrot. Simmer for at least 30 minutes. Serve with fresh basil.

Serves 4

Roasted Pepper Pesto

2 large red bell peppers

2 large yellow bell peppers

¾ cup (185 ml) **extra-virgin olive oil**

10 cloves garlic

1 tbsp sea salt

½ tbsp freshly ground pepper

1 tbsp each minced fresh thyme, rosemary and sage

You can keep any amount of any kind of pesto in the freezer. When you are ready to use it, just remove the amount you need. The handiest method of freezing pesto is to store it in ice cube trays.

Wash the bell peppers and pat them dry with a clean towel. Cut each pepper in half, remove the seeds and lay them on a baking tray with the open sides down. Brush both sides of each pepper with olive oil. Set the oven on broil and bake the pepper for approximately 15 minutes or until the skins blister. Remove the peppers to a pot, cover the pot and refrigerate for 30 to 40 minutes.

In the meantime, heat the remainder of the oil in a large saucepan then add the whole garlic cloves and roast them until they are golden. Remove them from the heat and let cool.

Peel the skin off the bell peppers and place the peppers in a food processor. Add garlic, salt, pepper and herbs. Turn on the food processor and add the oil slowly. Blend well for approximately 5 minutes.

s o u r c e s

Artesian Acres
R.R.3
Lacombe, AB
LOC 1S0
Canada
403-782-5075
1-888-400-2842

Prairie Harvest Canada Ltd.
Edmonton, AB
T5L 0X3
Canada
780-454-4004
prairie@istar.ca

Eden Foods, Inc.
701 Tecumseh Road
Clinton, MI 49236
USA
517-456-7424
marketing@edenfoods.com

Gabriele Pasta Products
City of Industry, CA 91748
USA

Mrs. Leeper's Inc.
12455 Kerran Street, Suite 200
Poway, CA 92064-6855
USA
858-486-1101

Organic Food Products, Inc.
P.O. Box 550
Aptos, CA 95001-0550
USA
408-782-1133

Purity Foods Inc.
2871 W. Jolly Road
Okemos, MI 48864
USA
517-351-9231

Page 9 photo credits:
Grant Heilman Photography/
Image Network Inc.

First published in 1999 by
alive books
7436 Fraser Park Drive
Burnaby BC V5J 5B9
604–435–1919
800–661–0303

© 1999 by Fred Edrissi

Book Design: Paul Chau
Artwork: Terence Yeung
          Raymond Cheung
Photography: Edmond Fong

Editing: Paul Razzell
Copyediting: Julie Cheng
Food styling: Fred Edrissi

Canadian Cataloguing in
Publication Data

Edrissi, Fred, 1951–
  Chef's Healthy Pasta

Alive natural health guides, 2
ISSN 1490-6503
Includes index.
ISBN 1–55312–001–9

1. Cookery (Pasta)
2. Vegetarian cookery. I. Title. II. Series.
TX809.M17E37 1999
641.8'22   C99–910849–2

Printed in Canada

Revolutionary Health Books

alive Natural Health Guides

Each 64-page book focuses on a single subject, is written in easy-to-understand language and is lavishly illustrated with full color photographs.

New titles will be published every month in each of the four series.

Self Help Guides

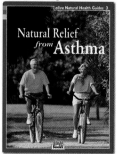

other titles to follow:

- **Nature's Own Candida Cure**
- **Natural Treatment for Chronic Fatigue Syndrome**
- **Fibromyalgia Be Gone!**
- **Heart Disease: Save Your Heart Naturally**
- **Liver Cleansing Diet**

Kitchen Guides

other titles to follow:

- **Baking with the Bread Machine**
- **Baking Bread: Delicious, Quick and Easy**
- **Healthy Breakfasts**
- **Salads and Salad Dressings**
- **Smoothies and Other Healthy Drinks**

Healing Foods & Herbs

other titles to follow:

- **Calendula: The Healthy Skin Helper**
- **Ginkgo Biloba: The Good Memory Herb**
- **Rhubarb and the Heart**
- **Saw Palmetto: The Key to Prostate Health**
- **St. John's Wort: Sunshine for Your Soul**

Lifestyle & Alternative Treatments

other titles to follow:

- **Maintain Health with Acupuncture**
- **The Complete Natural Cosmetics Book**
- **Kneipp Hydrotherapy at Home**
- **Magnetic Therapy and Natural Healing**
- **Sauna: Your Way to Better Health**

Vancouver
Canada

Great gifts at a great affordable price **$9.95 Cdn / $8.95 US / $11.95 Aust**

Natural Health Guides are available in bookstores and in health and nutrition centers.
For information or to place orders please dial 800-663-6580 or 800-661-0303